Altars
OF THE HEART
PERSONAL
MINISTRY GUIDE

Healing Wounded Emotions
in the Presence of God

D1519565

THOM GARDNER

Treasure House

An Imprint of

Destiny Image® Publishers, Inc.
P.O. Box 310
Shippensburg, PA 17257-0310

"For where your treasure is, there will your heart be also."
Matthew 6:21

ISBN 0-7684-3020-8

For Worldwide Distribution
Printed in the U.S.A.

This book and all other Destiny Image, Revival Press, MercyPlace, Fresh Bread, Destiny Image Fiction, and Treasure House books are available at Christian bookstores and distributors worldwide.

For a U.S. bookstore nearest you, call **1-800-722-6774**.
For more information on foreign distributors, call **717-532-3040**.
Or reach us on the Internet:

www.destinyimage.com

ABOUT THE PERSONAL MINISTRY GUIDE

This Personal Ministry Guide is a multipurpose companion for *Altars of the Heart*. First, it was written to help the reader understand and personally apply the teaching contained in the book. It also serves as the outline for the *Altars of the Heart Ministry Training Seminar*, which is offered in local churches to train Christian workers in the ministry of emotional healing. The Personal Ministry Guide contains some supplemental material that is not included in *Altars of the Heart*, and provides a way for readers to grow personally in their relationship with the Lord Himself through journaling their personal healing and revelation of God.

Each chapter of the Personal Ministry Guide is divided into three parts: Learning, Living, and Lighting. *Learning* summarizes the information in *Altars of the Heart* and also serves as the basic outline for the Ministry Seminar. (The author assumes that those taking the seminar have already read the entire text of the book.) This Personal Ministry Guide will be most useful to those who have read the text of *Altars of the Heart*.

The *Living* portion of each chapter provides an opportunity for personal application of what the reader has learned. It takes the teaching deeper into your life the experience allowing you to interact and apply the teaching of the book. You will be invited to be healed in a systematic and personal way.

The *Lighting* sections deal with your own new revelation of the character of God. The goal of healing is to remove obstacles to intimacy with God. When these obstacles are removed, new light is shed on the Person and character of God. You will be invited to share and chronicle your growing knowledge and love of God.

We invite you to take your time as you go through this material. The Lord longs to pour out his compassion on you and to bring you closer to Him. The emotional wounding you experienced was personal and so is the healing the Lord has for you.

CONTENTS

Part I

THE NEED FOR
HEALING WOUNDED EMOTIONS

Introduction

Learning

Reading assignment: Introduction, pages 11-13.

1. All of us have some kind of limp in our emotional lives.

    *   Limping in personal relationships
    *   Limping in our understanding of who we are
    *   Limping in our relationship with God Himself

2. The emotional limping and limitations in our lives come as the result of wrong ideas about our relationship with God.

    *   Ideas that came from past wounds, which David Seamands compares to annual growth rings in a tree[1]
    *   Ideas that came from family or cultural dysfunction
    *   Ideas that came from legalistic religion

3. God wants to bring us peace and healing so that He can bring us closer to Himself.

    But now in Christ Jesus you who formerly were far off have been brought near by the blood of Christ. For He Himself is our peace... (Ephesians 2:13-14).

4. It is God's intention to bring us to a place of peace through the atoning work of Jesus Christ. God is a restoring God—the "God of peace" who longs to heal us from the things that separate us from Him.

    *   The *God of peace* with be with you (Rom. 15:33; Phil. 4:9).
    *   The *God of peace* will crush satan under your feet (Rom. 16:20).

---

1. David A. Seamands, *Healing Damaged Emotions*, (Colorado Springs, CO; Cook Communications Ministries; 2002).

- The *God of peace* will set you apart for Himself (1 Thess. 5:23).
- The *God of peace* will bring you peace (2 Thess. 3:16).
- The *God of peace* will equip and empower you for life in Christ (Heb. 13:20).

Living

If you picked up *Altars of the Heart*, there is a good chance that you feel some kind of emotional limitation in your life—areas and issues where you limp. Maybe you limp in the area of personal relationships or perhaps you drag around feelings of unworthiness. Where do you limp in your life?

What kinds of nagging negative thoughts keep replaying in your head? It won't be hard to find them. They are the reason you picked up this book. Take a few minutes and write them down.

_____

_____

_____

_____

_____

As you think about the emotional limping in your life, the things you just wrote down, write down a recent event or time when you seem to notice your limp.

_____

_____

_____

_____

_____

What is your greatest frustration in relationships with other people?

_____

_____

_____

_____

_____

Describe your relationship with the Lord. Does God feel close or far away from you? Does God seem like a distant and disinterested father who comes home from work late and in a bad mood? Or does God seem more like a father who is involved in your life in a caring way? Maybe you are somewhere in between. Is God keeping score, or is He keeping watch over you?

_____

_____

_____

_____

_____

_____

Is the presence of God a warm or a scary thought for you? Why?

_____

_____

_____

_____

What do you long to hear from God?

_____

_____

_____

_____

Lighting

What have you learned about the heart of God toward you from the Introduction? Write it down along with any other thoughts.

_____

_____

_____

_____

_____

_____

_____

_____

_____

_____

_____

_____

_____

_____

_____

_____

_____

_____

_____

_____

Chapter One

A FULLER GOSPEL

Reading assignment: Chapter One, pages 17-24.

Learning

"When the Lord your God brings you into the land where you are entering to possess it..." (Deuteronomy 7:1).

1. God is taking us somewhere—bringing us into something. The "land" referred to here is a place where we dwell in peace and intimacy with God. There are things that prevent us from having that peace and intimacy with Him.

> "Many Christians are hounded by fear, rejection, worthlessness, shame, insecurity, defilement, hopelessness, or some combination of all of these. We may have a 'saving knowledge' that we are bound for Heaven, but at the same time we live out a kind of emotional hell on earth. Many in the Body of Christ have yet to experience their 're-birthright' in Jesus Christ. Although we *should* be living in the power and purpose of God, we instead limp from one day to the next waiting to go to Heaven. That is not God's idea. This is not all there is to life on earth. Why do we live so far below our position in Christ? The truth is that while we may know the gospel, we have yet to believe it!" (*Altars of the Heart*, p. 18)

2. Jesus told us that He came to bring us abundant life and that there are "thieves" (lies) who come to "steal, kill, and destroy" that abundant life in God.

"The thief comes only to steal and kill and destroy; I came that they may have life, and have it abundantly" (John 10:10).

3.   These thieves challenge our security and significance that is ours in Christ. The truth is that we are "chosen" and "loved" or "accepted" by God's grace in Christ Jesus (Eph. 1:3-6; Deut. 7:7).

> "We are 'secure' in the love of God and 'significant' in that God has *chosen* us.There can be no higher significance than to be chosen by the One who created us. Apart from our understanding that we are chosen or accepted by God, we will try all manner of things to achieve acceptability, most of which will end up wounding us further. On the other hand, out of the love and acceptance of God comes all that we could ever want or need for a whole and meaningful life. And that is where God is taking us—that is what He desires to 'bring us into' " (*Altars of the Heart*, p. 20).

4.   God's objective for your life is rest and peace, communion with Himself, and shared purpose in Christ (see Lev. 26:12).

•   Rest and peace
"So I have come down to deliver them from the power of the Egyptians, and to bring them up from that land to a good and spacious land, to a land flowing with milk and honey" (Ex. 3:8).

•   Communion with God
"I will also walk among you and be your God, and you shall be My people" (Lev. 26:12).

•   Shared purpose in Christ
"...for in Him we live and move and exist..." (Acts 17:28).

5.   God has prepared a place of wholeness in Christ.

•   When we feel fear...   Christ is with us.
•   When we feel rejected...   Christ accepts us.
•   When we feel worthless... Christ approves us.
•   When we feel shame...   Christ covers us.

- When we feel insecure…   Christ surrounds us.
- When we feel defiled…   Christ restores us.
- When we feel hopeless…   Christ becomes our living hope.

For God in all His fullness was pleased to live in Christ, and by Him God reconciled everything to Himself. He made peace with everything in heaven and on earth by means of His blood on the cross. This includes you who were once so far away from God. You were His enemies, separated from Him by your evil thoughts and actions, yet now He has brought you back as His friends. He has done this through His death on the cross in His own human body. As a result, He has brought you into the very presence of God, and you are holy and blameless as you stand before Him without a single fault (Colossians 1:19-22 NLT).

Living

What is it that you have a hard time believing or accepting about your relationship with God—your salvation—God's love and grace toward you through Christ?

_____

_____

_____

_____

_____

Where do you not feel loved or accepted in God? What kinds of things do you do to try to feel safe and secure?

_____

_____

_____

_____

_____

What do you think makes you valuable? What makes others more or less valuable than you? Be honest.

_____

_____

_____

_____

Where do you tend to squirm in God's lap trying to earn, figure out, or fix things or people? What kinds of things rob your rest and take up your thoughts?

_____

_____

_____

_____

_____

Lighting

What have you learned concerning the heart of God toward you? What has God been speaking to you in this chapter about His love for you and the healing He desires to take place?

_____

_____

_____

_____

_____

_____

_____

_____

_____

Chapter Two

LIVING THE LIES THAT BIND

Reading assignment: Chapter Two, pages 25-33.

Learning

1. The ministry of inner healing is the ministry of truth that overcomes the lies that rob us of the abundant life that is ours in Christ restoring our intimacy with God.

> "...truth, insofar as God is concerned, is that which is whole or in order. When God speaks truth, the result is order. He spoke a word, and worlds came into being. Psalm 33 says that He spoke the heavens into existence. Whatever God speaks brings order and the resulting peace or wholeness. This is the Hebrew concept of *shalom*, which is a state of wholeness or integrity. Christ was *shalom* incarnate bringing truth, order, and peace to the earth" (*Altars of the Heart*, p. 27).

2. Truth is what is true, real, dependable, powerful, whatever is of God. Therefore it is the ministry of Jesus Christ, the fullness of grace and truth.

    And the Word became flesh, and dwelt among us, and we saw His glory, glory as of the only begotten from the Father, full of grace and truth (John 1:14).

3. Lies that originated in satan, the "father of lies," have no power unless we believe them (see Gen. 3:1-5).

4. Each nation listed in Deuteronomy 7:1 represents a "greater and stronger" influence—an emotional influence based upon a wrong idea of God.

    ...and clears away many nations before you, the Hittites and the Girgashites and the Amorites and the Canaanites and the Perizzites and the Hivites and the Jebusites, seven nations greater and stronger than you (Deuteronomy 7:1).

    *   Hittites: *Fear*
    *   Girgashites: *Rejection*
    *   Amorites: *Worthlessness*
    *   Canaanites: *Shame*
    *   Perizzites: *Insecurity*
    *   Hivites: *Defilement*
    *   Jebusites: *Hopelessness*

    Each of these influences provokes a response.

    *   Fear makes us run and hide.
    *   Rejection makes us wander in restlessness.
    *   Worthlessness makes us perform to prove our worth.
    *   Shame makes us cover up weakness or sin.
    *   Insecurity makes us build up or compensate.
    *   Defilement makes us live in mourning.
    *   Hopelessness makes us quit.

5. We must lay aside the old "self" and be renewed in our minds (Col. 3:9-10; Rom. 12:2). It's up to us. God delivers the enemy before us, but we must destroy each lie. Ministry is not magic; it is a process.

6. The pattern of healing wounded emotions is: *Truth—Order—Peace.*

> "The sequence then is *truth*, which restores *order*, which then results in *peace* with God. This is the same process that brings wholeness and peace in our individual lives. We must be put back in order to find emotional wholeness. And we must hear the truth if we are to be put back in order." (*Altars of the Heart*, p. 27).

Living

We believe a lot of things that are not really true. These false beliefs may be the source of feelings associated with things like fear, rejection, worthlessness, shame, insecurity, defilement, or hopelessness. One or more of these may have a hold on us.

Where do you feel "disorder" in your life? Where do you not experience peace? Maybe it's in your church—your marriage—personal relationships—your family? Take time to pray about these "disorderly" places then list them below, beginning with what seems to be the strongest.

_____

_____

_____

_____

_____

_____

Discuss times and seasons in your life when you lacked peace. There are always times we dread such as family gatherings at holidays or Monday mornings at school. What have been the times or typical occasions that you have dreaded? Why have they been a source of dread to you?

_____

_____

_____

_____

_____

_____

Lighting

Think for a moment about those places where peace has been hard to come by that you described above. Put yourself in those places now with the eyes of your heart. See yourself there and now pray for the Lord to show you His presence in those places. Write down what you see—how the Lord interacts with you or expresses His presence to you. This is not a mental exercise, nor is it visualization. The Lord is *really* in those places! You have to see Him with spiritual eyes.

_____

_____

_____

_____

_____

_____

_____

What are you learning about the heart of God as He displays Himself to you?

_____

_____

_____

_____

_____

_____

_____

_____

_____

_____

_____

_____

Chapter Three

EMOTIONAL ECHOES

Reading assignment: Chapter Three, pages 35-41.

Learning

"Man is disturbed not by things, but by what he believes about them" (Paraphrased from Epictetus, a Stoic philosopher).

> "All of us have experienced some kind of controlling emotional echo, whether it was loud or barely audible. These echoes control us in the sense that they cause us to act in ways that the world would see as irrational or out of proportion. There may be times when the slightest provocation causes us to blow up in anger or shrink back in terror. We know when we are under these echoes' control because our emotional response is out of balance with what is happening around us" (*Altars of the Heart*, p. 36).

1. There are "sounds" we hear today that bounce off previous experience and echo back the emotions felt in the original event.

2. There is a relationship between what we *feel* and what we *believe*. Our emotions are not based on what is absolutely true, but what feels true to us. What we *feel* is the product of what we *believe*, and what we believe is a product of what we have *experienced*. The order is *experience—beliefs—feelings*.

3. The experiences that shape what we believe and what we feel today may come from several sources. These experiences may be the result of traumatic wounds or abuse; they may come from the family

in which we were raised, or the culture that surrounds us, or sin that has not been dealt with.

4.   Though we did not acknowledge Him, God was there on the scene of the wounding or when lies were planted from our family culture or other sources that are reflected in emotional echoes today. He will silence the echoes as He brings us the awareness of His presence and His truth.

I pray that the eyes of your heart may be enlightened, so that you will know what is the hope of His calling, what are the riches of the glory of His inheritance in the saints, and what is the surpassing greatness of His power toward us who believe. These are in accordance with the working of the strength of His might which He brought about in Christ, when He raised Him from the dead and seated Him at His right hand in the heavenly places, far above all rule and authority and power and dominion, and every name that is named, not only in this age but also in the one to come. And He put all things in subjection under His feet, and gave Him as head over all things to the church, which is His body, the fullness of Him who fills all in all (Ephesians 1:18-23).

Living

We generally know when we are under the influence of some kind of emotional echo because our emotional responses seem to be out of proportion with the reality of what is happening around us. Where have you experienced emotions that seem to be out of balance? Give a recent or a typical example. What happened and how did you respond to it?

_____

_____

_____

_____

_____

_____

What kinds of events or circumstances have shaped your life today? For example: if you grew up in a home that did not express love, you might have trouble expressing love today. Look at each of the areas mentioned below and write out some of the factors or experiences that stand out to you that shaped your beliefs.

From traumatic events or wounds...

_____

_____

_____

_____

_____

From your birth family...

_____

_____

_____

_____

From the culture in which you were raised...

_____

_____

_____

_____

From sin that has not been dealt with...

_____

_____

_____

_____

_____

To help you see the connection with the emotional echo, consider the following scenario.

You are standing at your kitchen sink washing a few dishes after dinner. Suddenly, one of your best plates slips out of your hand and falls to the floor and shatters. What is the first thing you say to yourself?

_____

_____

_____

_____

_____

Where did you hear those words spoken before? Who said them and when?

_____

_____

_____

_____

_____

_____

Invite the presence of the Lord into the place where you remembered hearing those kinds of words and ask Him what He thinks about that memory frame.

The Lord said

"_____

_____

_____

_____

_____

_____"

Lighting

The Lord may already be expressing His presence in hurtful memories or circumstances as you have considered the various sources (family, culture, etc.). What have you learned about the heart and the intention of God to bring you healing and to silence the emotional echoes that reverberate in your present life? What, if anything, has the Lord spoken to you about those formative circumstances or traumas that resulted in emotional wounds?

_____

_____

_____

_____

_____

_____

_____

_____

_____

_____

_____

_____

_____

_____

_____

_____

_____

_____

Chapter Four

Tearing Down Altars

Reading assignment: Chapter Four, pages 43-56.

Learning

But thus you shall do to them: you shall tear down their altars, and smash their sacred pillars, and hew down their Asherim, and burn their graven images with fire (Deuteronomy 7:5).

> "As Moses and Israel prepared to cross into the place of peace and abundance that God had prepared for them, God gave them specific instructions on how to eliminate the influences that could keep them from enjoying the peace and rest He had provided for them. These nations represented influences like *fear, rejection, worthlessness, shame, insecurity, defilement,* and *hopelessness.* The Lord gave His people instructions for the destruction of these nations and the influences they represented" (*Altars of the Heart*, p. 43).

1. The "instructions for destruction" God gave to Moses told them to...

    *   "Tear down their *altars*." Locate and dismantle the pagan influences.
    *   "Smash their sacred *pillars*." Get rid of the things that remind them of those pagan influences.
    *   "Hew down their *Asherim*." Find and uncover places of darkness where these influences live.
    *   "Burn their graven images with *fire*." Purify and get rid of the false images or lies about God and all that those images represent.

2.   The instruction God gave to Moses reflects the process we follow today to seek out and destroy the lies and controlling emotional influences that stem from past inner wounds.

Altars—An altar represents *what* we feel today, or what controls us (such as fear, etc.).

Pillars—A pillar represents an emotional echo or triggering event that causes us to feel what we feel. Pillars are *when* we feel what we feel.

Asherim—Asherim represents the hidden dark place in the past *where* the lie was first planted.

Fire—Fire represents the presence and the *truth* of God that destroys the lies we have believed and have controlled us.

3.   God's instructions

- *"Tear down their altars…"* The Hebrew word *nathats* suggests that the altars of influence were built up one stone at a time and now must be torn down the same way. These have gained influence over a period of time and will be torn down a stone at a time.
- *"Smash sacred pillars…"* The Hebrew word *shabar*, translated "smash," suggests that we are removing the association with other lies and past wounds of those things in the present. We are removing the trigger by submitting it to the truth.
- *"Hew down their Asherim…"* Gadah, the Hebrew word for "hew," means that we must "destroy," to uncover the secret and dark places where the lies are embedded in our lives.
- *"Burn* [to purify] *their graven images with fire…"* Saraph, translated "burn," suggests that we submit lies to the truth of God's presence and word, thus destroying them.

Psalm 19:7-9 tell us about the character and effects of God's voice. Truth brings…

- Wholeness and restoration
- Understanding from God's perspective or wisdom
- Confidence and rejoicing
- Clarity and enlightenment of God's presence
- Purity and eternal value
- Sweetness of God's presence

4. God may speak to us through various ways. He expresses His presence through words, pictures, sensations, or His appearance in the memory.

    - When we feel fear, He shows Himself *with* us.
    - When we feel rejected, He accepts us with open arms.
    - When we feel worthless, He stands behind us in approval.
    - When we feel shame, He clothes and covers us.
    - When we feel insecure, He surrounds or embraces us.
    - When we feel defiled, He washes and restores us.
    - When we feel hopeless, He leads us to repentance and new understanding.

Living

The first step to finding emotional wholeness is to find out what it is that binds us. Fill out the Emotional Profile on the following page, totaling the columns. This survey is not the final word on what influences your life, but will help you to identify and perhaps clarify factors that sometimes affect your life and relationship with God.

_____

_____

_____

_____

_____

_____

_____

_____

_____

_____

_____

_____

EMOTIONAL PROFILE

If the words in the columns describe something you feel a lot, enter a **3**. If it is something you feel sometimes, enter a **2**. If it is seldom of never enter a **1**.

Hittites/Fear
"I'm alone."
____ Alone
____ Afraid
____ Paralyzed
____ Uneasy
____ Nervous
____ Terrified
____ Suspicious
____ Very cautious
____ Indecisive
____ Worried
____ **Total**
____ **Run**

Girgashites/Rejection
"I don't belong."
____ Separated
____ Angry
____ Rejected
____ Restless
____ Forgotten
____ Forsaken
____ Unwanted
____ Nameless
____ Left out
____ Confused
____ **Total**
____ **Wander**

Amorites/Worthlessness
"I'm not as good as…"
____ Unnoticed
____ Unattached
____ Ordinary
____ Unapproved
____ Jealous
____ Insignificant
____ Not as good as…
____ Unimportant
____ Unloved
____ Worthless
____ **Total**
____ **Perform**

Canaanites/Shame
"I am not good enough."
____ Ashamed
____ Condemned
____ Falling short
____ Beyond forgiveness
____ Failure
____ Foolish
____ Guilty
____ Embarrassed
____ Perfectionistic
____ Self-conscious
____ **Total**
____ **Cover**

Perrezites/Insecurity
"I am not safe."
____ Anxious
____ Volatile
____ Defensive
____ Controlled
____ Threatened
____ Distrustful
____ Isolated
____ Helpless
____ Overwhelmed
____ Trapped
____ **Total**
____ **Control**

Hivites/Defilement
"I am ruined for life."
____ Betrayed
____ Damaged
____ Dirty
____ Ruined
____ Dishonored
____ Stained
____ Discarded
____ Unclean
____ Useless
____ Violated
____ **Total**
____ **Mourn**

Jebusites/Hopelessness
"I will never…"
____ Cursed
____ Defeated
____ Depressed
____ Negative
____ Tired
____ Empty
____ Indifferent
____ Pessimistic
____ Suicidal
____ Disappointed
____ **Total**
____ **Quit**

What words stand out? Are there other words that describe how you feel?

This is not an absolute picture of your emotional profile. These are certainly not the only words that could have been used to describe what we feel. Look at the strongest responses and see how they may compare to the emotional portraits in the various emotion chapters. Some words could fit in more than one column. This is just a way to look at all the emotional portraits at once. It is not scientific (neither are you). The words at the bottom of the columns, i.e. run, Wander, etc., describe the effects of the various emotional influences. They describe the motion of your life and may be more indicative of the real issues that control your life.

What kinds of words stood out to you from the emotional survey? Are there words that better describe what you feel most of the time? List them here.

_____

_____

_____

_____

_____

_____

_____

_____

Lighting

God is determined to help us remove obstacles that keep us from knowing Him better. What is being revealed to you about God's love for you as you move toward healing? How is your image of God changing as you work through this book?

_____

_____

_____

_____

_____

_____

God longs for you to know how much He loves you—how much He has always loved you. Close your eyes and acknowledge the presence of the Lord as you write in this book. How do you see God expressing His love for you? Write whatever He seems to be showing you without trying to make it into a mental exercise. Let the eyes of your heart see Him. What do you see?

_____

_____

_____

_____

_____

_____

_____

_____

_____

_____

_____

_____

_____

_____

_____

_____

_____

_____

_____

_____

Chapter Five

LOOKING BOTH WAYS

Reading assignment: Chapter Five, pages 57-63.

Learning

O Lord, You have searched me and known me. You know when I sit down and when I rise up; You understand my thought from afar. You scrutinize my path and my lying down, and are intimately acquainted with all my ways. Even before there is a word on my tongue, behold, O Lord, You know it all. You have enclosed me behind and before, and laid Your hand upon me. Such knowledge is too wonderful for me; it is too high, I cannot attain to it (Psalm 139:1-6).

> "When we begin the inner-healing process, we are crossing over from lies to truth, from wounds to healing. In this crossing, we have a Father who takes our little, powerless hand into His strong hand and He looks both ways before we cross. The Father looks to the left, our past, and then to the right, our future, and in the safety of His grip, the present, we cross over to healing. Because our heavenly Father is bigger than we are, He can see infinitely in both directions and knows exactly where He's going. Nothing takes Him by surprise. We can trust His grip on our hand—we can feel it as we cross over. Father will not leave us alone as we find healing" (*Altars of the Heart*, p. 57).

1. God knows us—our past—our present—our future.

2. Everything we are and everything we have experienced is in the hand of God, including past wounds. God's knowing hand is like an

x-ray, which we cannot see, but which looks into the deepest parts of us to find injury and brokenness.

3.   His hand is behind us in the past—His hand is before us in the future—His hand is upon us in the present. God lives outside the boundaries of time and space; He is present everywhere and all the time at every instant. The Bible gives us a fuller idea of God's omnipresent perspective (see Ps. 90:4; 2 Pet. 3:8).

...I am God, and there is no other; I am God, and there is no one like Me, declaring the end from the beginning, and from ancient times things which have not been done...(Isaiah 46:9-10).

4.   The reality is that *God is still alive in the past to bring us healing.* God was there and is *still* there in that place where we were wounded, or where a lie was planted, whether or not we were aware of Him.

5.   There is nowhere we can go away from God's presence; not even the past. *"Where can I go from Your Spirit? Or where can I flee from Your presence?"* (Ps. 139: 7) God is here and there.

6.   As we go into the process of inner healing, allowing God's hand to search us, He will remind us of times of wounding then remind us of these painful memory pictures to bring truth and to heal the wounds they contain.

O God, You have searched me and You know me. Keep on searching me and knowing me. I will know You better as Your hand holds my hand, directing and healing me. In all times and in all places, Lord, don't let me go. (Based upon Psalm 139:23-24.)

Living

God has clearly told us that there is nowhere we can go from His presence, yet we do not always recognize His presence and involvement. These may be places of great pain or traumatic events, or may involve sins we have already repented and been forgiven of. What are some places where you have a hard time seeing the presence and involvement of God? Where do you feel that the Lord let go of your hand? Write down any of these places along with the reasons why you have trouble recognizing God's involvement.

_____

_____

_____

_____

_____

_____

At the end of Psalm 139 David invited God to keep searching him and finding anxious thoughts that needed to be healed. What are some places that you are reluctant to yield to the loving and searching hand that formed you? What places would you just as soon remain in the back of the closet?

_____

_____

_____

_____

_____

_____

_____

Lighting

What have you learned about the heart of God as you have gone through this chapter? Read all of Psalm 139 again and complete the following thoughts.

Because the Lord really knows me so well...

_____

_____

_____

_____

_____

Because the Lord's hand is in my past and future…

_____
_____
_____
_____
_____
_____

Because the Lord is with me everywhere and at all times, even when I see only darkness…

_____
_____
_____
_____
_____
_____

Because the Lord's hand has formed me and He calls me wonderful…

_____
_____
_____
_____
_____
_____

Write down any visions or images that come to your mind as you read Psalm 139. How do you see the presence of the Lord involved in your life now?

_____

_____

_____

_____

_____

_____

_____

_____

_____

_____

_____

_____

_____

_____

_____

_____

_____

_____

_____

_____

_____

_____

Part II

INSTRUCTIONS FOR PART II

If you are working through this book on your own, it is important that you have read the entire text of *Altars of the Heart*. The book is designed to help you experience and understand the emotions you feel and to become familiar with the biblical truth surrounding those issues. Take your time to work through these seven emotional issues slowly. This is a Spirit-led approach to healing wounded emotions, not a cognitive exercise to be mastered. Above all, the Lord wants to speak to you in these next pages. Listen softly for Him—respond to His gentle invitation to healing. Be led by the Spirit to the lap of your Father as the child of God that you truly are (see Rom. 8:14-16).

The "Learning" section for each of the seven emotions is intentionally brief and is intended only to serve as a kind of review outline of the content of the book itself. Again, it is important that you read the whole text of *Altars of the Heart* and experience these emotions along with the teaching in each of the seven chapters on the various influences and the emotions that result.

Chapter Six

Are You Afraid of the Dark?

Hittites: The Influence of Fear

Reading assignment: Chapter Six, pages 67-78.

Please read the Scripture text, First Kings 19:1-12, if you have not already done so.

Learning

1. The chief lie of the influence of fear is "*I am alone.*" Fear is the first emotion mentioned in the Bible and the most powerful (see Gen. 3:10).

2. Fear is the result of facing the world separated from the power and presence of God.

3. People who live under the influence of fear frequently feel…

   • Alone
   • Afraid
   • Paralyzed
   • Uneasy
   • Nervous
   • Terrified
   • Suspicious
   • Cautious
   • Indecisive
   • Worried

There may be other similar words that describe how we feel under this influence.

4. The effect of fear is that it makes us want to run away.

5. The truth about fear is that we are not alone. Immanuel, God is *with* us!

- *"My presence shall go with you, and I will give you rest"* (Ex. 33:14).
- *"I will be with you; I will not fail you or forsake you"* (Josh. 1:5b).
- *"Even though I walk through the valley of the shadow of death, I fear no evil, for You are with me"* (Ps. 23:4).
- *"Do not fear, for I am with you; do not anxiously look about you, for I am your God"* (Is. 41:10).
- *"When you pass through the waters, I will be with you"* (Is. 43:2).
- *"I will ask the Father, and He will give you another Helper, that He may be with you forever"* (Jn. 14:16).

Living

Step 1: What do you feel?

How does your life look like Elijah's did on Mt. Horeb? Do you feel alone, afraid, paralyzed, uneasy, nervous, terrified, suspicious, cautious, indecisive, and worried? Describe similarities of your life and Elijah's experience in the box below.

```
_____

_____

_____

_____

_____

_____
```

Step 2: When do you feel it?

Can you describe a recent time when you felt the things described above? Write a brief description in the picture frame below. Before you begin to write, acknowledge the presence and involvement of God through prayer. Do not proceed until you have bathed in prayer and His presence. Declare the intention of the Lord to bring you truth and healing and forbid any lies or interference from unclean spirits.

Describe what you were feeling in that recent event.

Step 3: Where did these feelings come from?

Now, pray that the Lord would lead you to the source of those feelings. Ask Him to take you by the hand and lead you to a memory that feels like the recent event you described. Describe the memory picture in the frame below as you did with the recent event. (Note that there may be more than one. Try to find the oldest memory or the one that stands out the most.)

As you look at the memory frame, ask the Lord to fill it with His presence. Don't move on to the next step until you have begun to experience the presence of God in this frame.

Step 4: What is the truth?

Once you have begun to experience the presence of God, ask yourself the following questions.

- *What* do you feel as you look at this memory frame?

As I look at this memory frame I feel…

_____

_____

_____

_____

- *Why* do you feel that way? The "*why*" is the lie.

I feel what I feel because…

_____

_____

_____

_____

Ask the Lord to *express* His presence in that memory frame. Describe how you experience the presence of the Lord (i.e. feelings, impressions, pictures, etc.). One easy way to do this is to see the memory frame as a painting. How is the Lord painting Himself into the picture? What is He doing—saying—expressing—gesturing to you as you focus on Him?

_____

_____

_____

_____

What does the Lord seem to be telling you about the truth of that situation through the expression of His presence, words, feelings, pictures, etc.?

I felt _____

because I believed _____.

But the truth is _____.

- Clean the house. Forgive or receive forgiveness associated with the memory. Forgive and release those who wounded you. (Remember that forgiveness is not an act of emotion, but an act of the will so that the pain of that memory can no longer control you.) Speak to them as though you and they are still in that old memory frame. Confess and receive forgiveness for any sin you are responsible for.
- Tell them what they did or said.
- Tell them what their actions or words caused you to believe that was not true.
- Tell them the truth that you have now heard from the Lord Himself.

How do you see those who wounded you in the memory frame now in relation to the Lord's presence? Describe it here.

_____

_____

_____

_____

Now revisit the recent situation you cited at the beginning of this exercise. How do you see it now in light of what God has shown you?

_____

_____

_____

_____

Now that you have received truth and healing, past and present, command all unclean spirits who took advantage of open doors to depart in the name of Jesus Christ. Tell them the truth then tell them to go!

_____

_____

_____

_____

What was true in the past is true in the present and will be God's promise to you in the future.

The truth in the past was: _____

_____

The truth in the present is: _____

_____

God's promise to me for the future is: _____

_____

Lighting

What has the Lord revealed to you concerning His presence and healing truth that He brought to your wounded memories? Note how He expressed His presence to you in the memory picture. Write down what that expression has taught you about God.

_____

_____

_____

_____

_____

Choose one or more of the Scriptures listed at the end of the "Learning" section and personalize them by writing them out here, substituting your name in the text.

_____

_____

_____

_____

_____

Chapter Seven

What Is Your Name?

Girgashites: The Influence of Rejection

Reading assignment: Chapter Seven, pages 79-90.

Please read the Scripture texts, Mark 5:1-20 and Luke 8:26-35, now if you have not already done so.

Learning

1. The chief lie of rejection is *"I do not belong,"* or *"I am not accepted."* Rejection is a result of being separated from the unconditional love and acceptance of God.

2. Those who live under the influence of rejection frequently feel...

    *   Separated, excluded
    *   Angry
    *   Rejected
    *   Restless
    *   Forgotten
    *   Forsaken
    *   Unwanted
    *   Nameless
    *   Left out
    *   Confused

    There may be other similar words that also describe how we feel under the influence of rejection.

3. Some biblical examples of the rejected are: Cain, Esau, Saul, and the older brother of the prodigal son.

4. The truth about rejection is:

    *   The acceptance of God is not based on our performance but on His kindness and mercy.

But when the kindness of God our Savior and His love for mankind appeared, He saved us, not on the basis of deeds which we have done in righteousness, but according to His mercy, by the washing of regeneration and renewing by the Holy Spirit, whom He poured out upon us richly through Jesus Christ our Savior (Titus 3:4-6).

• Jesus took our rejection upon Himself (see Is. 53:3).
"My God, my God, why have You forsaken me? Far from my deliverance are the words of my groaning. O my God, I cry by day, but You do not answer; and by night, but I have no rest" (Ps. 22:1-2).

• We are accepted in Christ.
"All that the Father gives Me will come to Me, and the one who comes to Me I will certainly not cast out" (Jn. 6:37).
"He has made us accepted in the Beloved" (Eph. 1:6 NKJ).

• We have been brought near and accepted by the blood of Christ.
"...He made Him who knew no sin to be sin for us, that we might become the righteousness of God in Him" (2 Cor. 5:21 NKJ).

"I have been crucified with Christ; it is no longer I who live, but Christ lives in me; and the life which I now live in the flesh I live by faith in the Son of God, who loved me and gave Himself for me" (Gal. 2:20-21 NKJ).

Living

Step 1: What do you feel?

When do you feel the influence of rejection? When do you feel like you don't belong or like you are an outsider? Are there times you feel separated, excluded, angry, rejected, restless, forgotten, forsaken, unwanted, nameless, left out, or confused? Describe similarities of your life and Elijah's experience in the box below.

Step 2: When do you feel it?

Can you describe a recent time when you felt the things described above? Write a brief description in the picture frame below. Before you begin to write, acknowledge the presence and involvement of God through prayer. Do not proceed until you have bathed in prayer and His presence. Declare the intention of the Lord to bring you truth and healing and forbid any lies or interference from unclean spirits.

Describe what you were feeling in that recent event.

```
┌─────────────────────────────────────────────────────┐
│                                                       │
│      ─────────────────────────────────────────       │
│                                                       │
│      ─────────────────────────────────────────       │
│                                                       │
│      ─────────────────────────────────────────       │
│                                                       │
│      ─────────────────────────────────────────       │
│                                                       │
└─────────────────────────────────────────────────────┘
```

Step 3: Where did these feelings come from?

Now, pray that the Lord would lead you to the source of those feelings. Ask Him to take you by the hand and lead you to a memory that feels like the recent event you described. Describe the memory picture in the frame below as you did with the recent event. (Note that there may be more than one. Try to find the oldest memory or the one that stands out the most.)

```
┌─────────────────────────────────────────────────────┐
│                                                       │
│      ─────────────────────────────────────────       │
│                                                       │
│      ─────────────────────────────────────────       │
│                                                       │
│      ─────────────────────────────────────────       │
│                                                       │
│      ─────────────────────────────────────────       │
│                                                       │
└─────────────────────────────────────────────────────┘
```

As you look at the memory frame, ask the Lord to fill it with His presence. Don't move on to the next step until you have begun to experience the presence of God in this frame.

Step 4: What is the truth?

Once you have begun to experience the presence of God, ask yourself the following questions.

• *What* do you feel as you look at this memory frame?

As I look at this memory frame I feel…

_____

_____

_____

_____

• *Why* do you feel that way? The *"why"* is the lie.

I feel what I feel because…

_____

_____

_____

_____

Ask the Lord to *express* His presence in that memory frame. Describe how you experience the presence of the Lord (i.e. feelings, impressions, pictures, etc.). One easy way to do this is to see the memory frame as a painting. How is the Lord painting Himself into the picture? What is He doing—saying—expressing—gesturing to you as you focus on Him?

_____

_____

_____

_____

• What does the Lord seem to be telling you about the truth of that situation through the expression of His presence, words, feelings, pictures, etc.?

I felt _____

because I believed _____.

But the truth is _____.

- Clean the house. Forgive or receive forgiveness associated with the memory. Forgive and release those who wounded you. (Remember that forgiveness is not an act of emotion, but an act of the will so that the pain of that memory can no longer control you.) Speak to them as though you and they are still in that old memory frame. Confess and receive forgiveness for any sin you are responsible for.
- Tell them what they did or said.
- Tell them what their actions or words caused you to believe that was not true.
- Tell them the truth that you have now heard from the Lord Himself.

How do you see those who wounded you in the memory frame now in relation to the Lord's presence? Describe it here.

_____

_____

_____

_____

_____

Now revisit the recent situation you cited at the beginning of this exercise. How do you see it now in light of what God has shown you?

_____

_____

_____

_____

_____

Now that you have received truth and healing, past and present, command all unclean spirits who took advantage of open doors to depart in the name of Jesus Christ. Tell them the truth then tell them to go!

_____

_____

_____

_____

What was true in the past is true in the present and will be God's promise to you in the future.

The truth in the past was: _____

_____

The truth in the present is: _____

_____

God's promise to me for the future is: _____

_____

Lighting

What has the Lord revealed to you concerning His presence and healing truth that He brought to your wounded memories? Note how He expressed His presence to you in the memory picture. Write down what that expression has taught you about God.

_____

_____

_____

_____

_____

_____

_____

Choose one or more of the Scriptures listed at the end of the "Learning" section and personalize them by writing them out here, substituting your name in the text. Soak in the truth that God has spoken to you—make it real in your life.

_____

_____

_____

_____

_____

_____

_____

_____

_____

_____

_____

_____

_____

_____

_____

_____

_____

_____

_____

_____

_____

_____

Chapter Eight

LIVING IN SECOND PLACE

Amorites: The Influence of Worthlessness

Reading assignment: Chapter Eight, pages 91-102.

Please read the Scripture texts, Genesis 29:21-30:21, now if you have not already done so.

Learning

1. The chief lie associated with the influence of worthlessness is "I am not as good as…." When we live under the influence of worthlessness we compare ourselves to other people.

2. Those who live under the influence of worthlessness frequently feel… unnoticed, unattached, ordinary, unapproved, jealous, insignificant, not as good as, unimportant, unloved, or worthless. There may be other similar words that also describe how they feel.

3. The effect of worthlessness is that we are driven to perform.

4. The truth about worthlessness is…

    • God made us. We are His precious creations.

    • *"Know that the Lord Himself is God; it is He who has made us, and not we ourselves; we are His people and the sheep of His pasture"* (Ps. 100:3).

    • *"Thus says the Lord, your Redeemer, and the one who formed you from the womb, 'I, the Lord, am the maker of all things, stretching out the heavens by Myself and spreading out the earth all alone'"* (Is. 44:24).

    • *"For we are His workmanship, created in Christ Jesus for good works, which God prepared beforehand so that we would walk in them"* (Eph. 2:10).

- *"For You formed my inward parts; You wove me in my mother's womb. I will give thanks to You, for I am fearfully and wonderfully made; wonderful are Your works, and my soul knows it very well"* (Ps. 139:13-14).

Living

Step 1: What do you feel?

How does your life look like Leah's? Do you live in second place? Are you always working and striving to prove your value? Do you compare yourself to other people? Do you struggle with feelings of being unloved, unnoticed, unattached, jealous, unworthy, unapproved, ordinary, insignificant, not as good as, or unimportant? Describe similarities of your life and Leah's experience in the box below.

_____

_____

_____

_____

Step 2: When do you feel it?

Can you describe a recent time when you felt the things described above? Write a brief description in the picture frame below. Before you begin to write, acknowledge the presence and involvement of God through prayer. Do not proceed until you have bathed in prayer and His presence. Declare the intention of the Lord to bring you truth and healing and forbid any lies or interference from unclean spirits.

Describe what you were feeling in that recent event.

_____

_____

_____

_____

Step 3: Where did these feelings come from?

Now, pray that the Lord would lead you to the source of those feelings. Ask Him to take you by the hand and lead you to a memory that feels like the recent event you described. Describe the memory picture in the frame below as you did with the recent event. (Note that there may be more than one. Try to find the oldest memory or the one that stands out the most.)

> _____
>
> _____
>
> _____
>
> _____

As you look at the memory frame, ask the Lord to fill it with His presence. Don't move on to the next step until you have begun to experience the presence of God in this frame.

Step 4: What is the truth?

Once you have begun to experience the presence of God, ask yourself the following questions.

- ***What*** do you feel as you look at this memory frame?

As I look at this memory frame I feel…

_____

_____

_____

_____

- ***Why*** do you feel that way? The "*why*" is the lie.

I feel what I feel because…

_____

_____

_____

_____

Ask the Lord to *express* His presence in that memory frame. Describe how you experience the presence of the Lord (i.e. feelings, impressions, pictures, etc.). One easy way to do this is to see the memory frame as a painting. How is the Lord painting Himself into the picture? What is He doing—saying—expressing—gesturing to you as you focus on Him?

_____

_____

_____

_____

- What does the Lord seem to be telling you about the truth of that situation through the expression of His presence, words, feelings, pictures, etc.?

I felt _____

because I believed _____.

But the truth is _____.

- Clean the house. Forgive or receive forgiveness associated with the memory. Forgive and release those who wounded you. (Remember that forgiveness is not an act of emotion, but an act of the will so that the pain of that memory can no longer control you.) Speak to them as though you and they are still in that old memory frame. Confess and receive forgiveness for any sin you are responsible for.

- Tell them what they did or said.

- Tell them what their actions or words caused you to believe that was not true.

- Tell them the truth that you have now heard from the Lord Himself.

How do you see those who wounded you in the memory frame now in relation to the Lord's presence? Describe it here.

_____

_____

_____

_____

Now revisit the recent situation you cited at the beginning of this exercise. How do you see it now in light of what God has shown you?

_____

_____

_____

_____

Now that you have received truth and healing, past and present, command all unclean spirits who took advantage of open doors to depart in the name of Jesus Christ. Tell them the truth then tell them to go!

_____

_____

_____

_____

What was true in the past is true in the present and will be God's promise to you in the future.

The truth in the past was: _____

_____

The truth in the present is: _____

_____

God's promise to me for the future is: _____

_____

Lighting

What has the Lord revealed to you concerning His presence and healing truth that He brought to your wounded memories? Note how He expressed His presence to you in the memory picture. Write down what that expression has taught you about God.

_____

_____

_____

_____

_____

_____

_____

Choose one or more of the Scriptures listed at the end of the "Learning" section and personalize them by writing them out here, substituting your name in the text. Soak in the truth that God has spoken to you—make it real in your life.

_____

_____

_____

_____

_____

_____

_____

_____

_____

_____

Chapter Nine

CRYING OVER SPILLED MILK

Canaanites: The Influence of Shame

Reading assignment: Chapter Nine, pages 103-116.

Please read the Scripture text, Genesis 3:1-10, if you have not already done so.

Learning

1. The chief lie of shame is "I'm not good enough." Shame is the feeling that we fall short of someone's standard or expectations. Those who live under the influence of shame compare themselves to a standard, ideal, or expectation.

2. We feel shame because we are out of intimate contact with God. Before he fell, Adam was naked and not ashamed. Shame and nakedness go together (see Gen. 2:25).

3. Those who live under the influence of shame frequently feel...
   • Ashamed
   • Condemned
   • Falling short
   • Beyond forgiveness
   • Failure
   • Foolish
   • Guilty
   • Embarrassed
   • Perfectionistic
   • Self-conscious

There may be similar words that also describe how we feel when we live under shame.

4. The effect of shame is that we want to hide behind something or sew fig leaves together to cover our nakedness.

5.   The truth about shame:
   •   God calls us to restoration and grace. *"Then the Lord God called to the man, and said to him, 'Where are you?'"* (Gen. 3:9)
   •   He would carry our nakedness to the cross. Jesus was naked and not ashamed because of His relationship with the Father.
   •   The truth is that God is there and knows all. *"And there is no creature hidden from His sight, but all things are open and laid bare to the eyes of Him with whom we have to do"* (Heb. 4:13).
   •   Our nakedness does not separate us from God.

Who will separate us from the love of Christ? Will tribulation, or distress, or persecution, or famine, or nakedness, or peril, or sword?...For I am convinced that neither death, nor life, nor angels, nor principalities, nor things present, nor things to come, nor powers, nor height, nor depth, nor any other created thing, will be able to separate us from the love of God, which is in Christ Jesus our Lord (Romans 8:35, 38-39).

Living

Step 1: What do you feel?

How does the picture of Adam and Eve resemble your life? Do you sometimes feel ashamed, guilty, embarrassed, foolish, like a failure, self-conscious, perfectionistic, beyond forgiveness, guilty, or condemned? Do you feel as though you can't do enough or that you want to hide? Describe similarities of your life and those of Adam and Eve's experiences in the box below.

```
_____

_____

_____

_____
```

Step 2: When do you feel it?

Can you describe a recent time when you felt the things described above? Write a brief description in the picture frame below. Before you begin to write, acknowledge the presence and involvement of God through prayer. Do not proceed until you have bathed in prayer and His presence. Declare the intention of the Lord to bring you truth and healing and forbid any lies or interference from unclean spirits.

Describe what you were feeling in that recent event.

$$\begin{array}{|l|} \hline \\ \rule{9cm}{0.4pt} \\ \rule{9cm}{0.4pt} \\ \rule{9cm}{0.4pt} \\ \rule{9cm}{0.4pt} \\ \hline \end{array}$$

Step 3: Where did these feelings come from?

Now, pray that the Lord would lead you to the source of those feelings. Ask Him to take you by the hand and lead you to a memory that feels like the recent event you described. Describe the memory picture in the frame below as you did with the recent event. (Note that there may be more than one. Try to find the oldest memory or the one that stands out the most.)

$$\begin{array}{|l|} \hline \\ \rule{9cm}{0.4pt} \\ \rule{9cm}{0.4pt} \\ \rule{9cm}{0.4pt} \\ \rule{9cm}{0.4pt} \\ \hline \end{array}$$

As you look at the memory frame, ask the Lord to fill it with His presence. Don't move on to the next step until you have begun to experience the presence of God in this frame.

Step 4: What is the truth?

Once you have begun to experience the presence of God, ask yourself the following questions.

• *What* do you feel as you look at this memory frame?

As I look at this memory frame I feel...

_____

_____

_____

_____

•   **Why** do you feel that way? The "*why*" is the lie.

I feel what I feel because…

_____

_____

_____

_____

Ask the Lord to *express* His presence in that memory frame. Describe how you experience the presence of the Lord (i.e. feelings, impressions, pictures, etc.). One easy way to do this is to see the memory frame as a painting. How is the Lord painting Himself into the picture? What is He doing—saying—expressing—gesturing to you as you focus on Him?

_____

_____

_____

_____

•   What does the Lord seem to be telling you about the truth of that situation through the expression of His presence, words, feelings, pictures, etc.?

I felt _____

because I believed _____.

But the truth is _____.

•   Clean the house. Forgive or receive forgiveness associated with the memory. Forgive and release those who wounded you. (Remember that forgiveness is not an act of emotion, but an act of the will so that the pain of that memory can no longer control you.) Speak to them as though you and they are still in that old memory frame. Confess and receive forgiveness for any sin you are responsible for.

- Tell them what they did or said.

- Tell them what their actions or words caused you to believe that was not true.

- Tell them the truth that you have now heard from the Lord Himself.

How do you see those who wounded you in the memory frame now in relation to the Lord's presence? Describe it here.

_____

_____

_____

_____

_____

Now revisit the recent situation you cited at the beginning of this exercise. How do you see it now in light of what God has shown you?

_____

_____

_____

_____

Now that you have received truth and healing, past and present, command all unclean spirits who took advantage of open doors to depart in the name of Jesus Christ. Tell them the truth then tell them to go!

_____

_____

_____

_____

What was true in the past is true in the present and will be God's promise to you in the future.

The truth in the past was: _____

_____

The truth in the present is: _____

_____

God's promise to me for the future is: _____

_____

Lighting

What has the Lord revealed to you concerning His presence and healing truth that He brought to your wounded memories? Note how He expressed His presence to you in the memory picture. Write down what that expression has taught you about God.

_____

_____

_____

_____

_____

_____

Choose one or more of the Scriptures listed at the end of the "Learning" section and personalize them by writing them out here, substituting your name in the text. Soak in the truth that God has spoken to you—make it real in your life.

_____

_____

_____

_____

_____

_____

Chapter Ten

LIVING ON THE LEDGE

Perizzites: Insecurity

Reading assignment: Chapter Ten, pages 117-130.

Please read the Scripture text, Second Samuel 9:3-5, if you have not already done so.

Learning

1. The chief lie of insecurity is "I am helpless, unprotected." It is a state of living without walls, insecurity or vulnerability. Many times the insecure have been abused people who feel unprotected.

2. To be insecure is to live with a feeling of being unprotected, unsafe, powerless or distracted. The insecure spend their time crunched up in a ball of self-protection and seldom get close to or trust anyone. They "live on the ledge" watching for the next attack. The lie of insecurity is that everything is a threat.

3. Those who live under the influence of insecurity frequently feel...

    *   Anxious
    *   Volatile
    *   Defensive
    *   Controlled
    *   Threatened
    *   Distrustful
    *   Isolated
    *   Helpless
    *   Overwhelmed
    *   Cornered or trapped

    There may be similar or better words to describe how you feel.

4. The truth about insecurity
    *   We are loved perfectly by the most secure Person in the universe. *"Perfect love casts out fear"* (1 Jn. 4:18).
    *   We are safe in God's grace that flows from His total security. Psalm 27:1 (NLT) says: *"The Lord is my light and my salvation—so why should I be afraid? The Lord protects me from danger—so why should I tremble?"*
    *   We live at God's table. *"You prepare a table before me in the presence of my enemies; You have anointed my head with oil; my cup overflows"* (Ps. 23:5).
    *   Our lameness is under the King's table, just as Mephibosheth's legs. We can extend grace to others who also need to sit at the table. It is not our table but the King's—not our grace but the Lord's.
    *   We are surrounded by God.

For it is You who blesses the righteous man, O Lord, You surround him with favor as with a shield (Ps. 5:12).

Those who trust in the Lord are as Mount Zion, which cannot be moved but abides forever. As the mountains surround Jerusalem, so the Lord surrounds His people from this time forth and forever (Ps. 125:1-2).

But You, O Lord, are a shield about me, my glory, and the One who lifts my head (Ps. 3:3).

Many are the sorrows of the wicked, but he who trusts in the Lord, lovingkindness shall surround him (Ps. 32:10).

Living

Step 1: What do you feel?

How does the picture of Mephibosheth's life on the ledge compare with your life? Are there times when you feel unsafe, threatened, controlled, volatile, helpless, defensive, distrustful, isolated, anxious, or overwhelmed—like it's you against the world? Describe similarities of your life and the experiences of Mephibosheth in the box below.

_____

_____

_____

_____

_____

Step 2: When do you feel it?

Can you describe a recent time when you felt the things described above? Write a brief description in the picture frame below. Before you begin to write, acknowledge the presence and involvement of God through prayer. Do not proceed until you have bathed in prayer and His presence. Declare the intention of the Lord to bring you truth and healing and forbid any lies or interference from unclean spirits.

Describe what you were feeling in that recent event.

_____

_____

_____

_____

Step 3: Where did these feelings come from?

Now, pray that the Lord would lead you to the source of those feelings. Ask Him to take you by the hand and lead you to a memory that feels like the recent event you described. Describe the memory picture in the frame below as you did with the recent event. (Note that there may be more than one. Try to find the oldest memory or the one that stands out the most.)

_____

_____

_____

_____

As you look at the memory frame, ask the Lord to fill it with His presence. Don't move on to the next step until you have begun to experience the presence of God in this frame.

Step 4: What is the truth?

Once you have begun to experience the presence of God, ask yourself the following questions.

- *What* do you feel as you look at this memory frame?

As I look at this memory frame I feel...

_____

_____

_____

_____

- *Why* do you feel that way? The "*why*" is the lie.

I feel what I feel because...

_____

_____

_____

_____

Ask the Lord to *express* His presence in that memory frame. Describe how you experience the presence of the Lord (i.e. feelings, impressions, pictures, etc.). One easy way to do this is to see the memory frame as a painting. How is the Lord painting Himself into the picture? What is He doing—saying—expressing—gesturing to you as you focus on Him?

_____

_____

_____

_____

- What does the Lord seem to be telling you about the truth of that situation through the expression of His presence, words, feelings, pictures, etc.?

I felt _____

because I believed _____.

But the truth is _____.

- Clean the house. Forgive or receive forgiveness associated with the memory. Forgive and release those who wounded you. (Remember that forgiveness is not an act of emotion, but an act of the will so that the pain of that memory can no longer control you.) Speak to them as though you and they are still in that old memory frame. Confess and receive forgiveness for any sin you are responsible for.
- Tell them what they did or said.
- Tell them what their actions or words caused you to believe that was not true.
- Tell them the truth that you have now heard from the Lord Himself.

How do you see those who wounded you in the memory frame now in relation to the Lord's presence? Describe it here.

_____

_____

_____

_____

_____

Now revisit the recent situation you cited at the beginning of this exercise. How do you see it now in light of what God has shown you?

_____

_____

_____

_____

_____

Now that you have received truth and healing, past and present, command all unclean spirits who took advantage of open doors to depart in the name of Jesus Christ. Tell them the truth then tell them to go!

_____

_____

_____

_____

What was true in the past is true in the present and will be God's promise to you in the future.

The truth in the past was: _____

_____

The truth in the present is: _____

_____

God's promise to me for the future is: _____

_____

Lighting

What has the Lord revealed to you concerning His presence and healing truth that He brought to your wounded memories? Note how He expressed His presence to you in the memory picture. Write down what that expression has taught you about God.

_____

_____

_____

_____

_____

_____

_____

Choose one or more of the Scriptures listed at the end of the "Learning" section and personalize them by writing them out here, substituting your name in the text. Soak in the truth that God has spoken to you—make it real in your life.

_____

_____

_____

_____

_____

_____

_____

_____

_____

_____

_____

_____

_____

_____

_____

_____

_____

_____

_____

_____

_____

_____

Chapter Eleven

Torn Sleeves

Hivites: Defilement

Reading assignment: Chapter Eleven, pages 131-141.

Please read the Scripture text, Second Samuel 13:1-19, if you have not already done so.

Learning

1. The chief lie of defilement is *"I am ruined for life."* To be defiled means to take something pure and make it unclean or polluted.

2. Defilement happens when an innocent and trusting victim is overpowered or violated by force.

3. There is a sense of betrayal by the ones who should be safe for us.

4. Those who live under the influence of defilement frequently feel…

   - Betrayed
   - Damaged
   - Dirty
   - Ruined
   - Dishonored
   - Stained
   - Discarded
   - Unclean
   - Useless
   - Violated

   There may be other similar words that describe how you feel.

5. The effect of defilement is that we spend our lives mourning our betrayal and lost innocence.

6. The truth about defilement.

- It was not your fault. It was someone else's sin against you.

But if in the field the man finds the girl who is engaged, and the man forces her and lies with her, then only the man who lies with her shall die. But you shall do nothing to the girl; there is no sin in the girl worthy of death, for just as a man rises against his neighbor and murders him, so is this case (Deut. 22:25-26).

- God was there with you, even though you did not recognize His presence. It was not His desire for you to be abused, but to be washed and restored.

"When I passed by you and saw you squirming in your blood, I said to you while you were in your blood, 'Live!' Yes, I said to you while you were in your blood, 'Live!'…so I spread My skirt over you and covered your nakedness. I also swore to you and entered into a covenant with you so that you became Mine," declares the Lord God. "Then I bathed you with water, washed off your blood from you and anointed you with oil. I also clothed you with embroidered cloth and put sandals of porpoise skin on your feet; and I wrapped you with fine linen and covered you with silk. ..you were exceedingly beautiful and advanced to royalty" (Ezekiel 16:6-13).

- Life is not over—God will restore and rebuild.

Also I will restore the captivity of My people Israel, and they will rebuild the ruined cities and live in them; they will also plant vineyards and drink their wine, and make gardens and eat their fruit (Amos 9:14).

Living

Step 1: What do you feel?

How does the picture of Tamar's experience compare with yours? When do you feel betrayed, confused, violated, damaged, shameful, dirty, ruined, spoiled, unclean, useless, or anything similar to these emotions? Have you lived in mourning? Describe similarities of your life and experiences of Tamar in the box below.

_____

_____

Step 2: When do you feel it?

Can you describe a recent time when you felt the things described above? Write a brief description in the picture frame below. Before you begin to write, acknowledge the presence and involvement of God through prayer. Do not proceed until you have bathed in prayer and His presence. Declare the intention of the Lord to bring you truth and healing and forbid any lies or interference from unclean spirits.

Describe what you were feeling in that recent event.

_____

_____

_____

_____

_____

Step 3: Where did these feelings come from?

Now, pray that the Lord would lead you to the source of those feelings. Ask Him to take you by the hand and lead you to a memory that feels like the recent event you described. Describe the memory picture in the frame below as you did with the recent event. (Note that there may be more than one. Try to find the oldest memory or the one that stands out the most.)

_____

_____

_____

_____

_____

As you look at the memory frame, ask the Lord to fill it with His presence. Don't move on to the next step until you have begun to experience the presence of God in this frame.

Step 4: What is the truth?

Once you have begun to experience the presence of God, ask yourself the following questions.

• *What* do you feel as you look at this memory frame?

As I look at this memory frame I feel...

_____

_____

_____

_____

• *Why* do you feel that way? The "*why*" is the lie.

I feel what I feel because...

_____

_____

_____

_____

Ask the Lord to *express* His presence in that memory frame. Describe how you experience the presence of the Lord (i.e. feelings, impressions, pictures, etc.). One easy way to do this is to see the memory frame as a painting. How is the Lord painting Himself into the picture? What is He doing—saying—expressing—gesturing to you as you focus on Him?

_____

_____

_____

_____

- What does the Lord seem to be telling you about the truth of that situation through the expression of His presence, words, feelings, pictures, etc.?

I felt _____

because I believed _____ .

But the truth is _____ .

- Clean the house. Forgive or receive forgiveness associated with the memory. Forgive and release those who wounded you. (Remember that forgiveness is not an act of emotion, but an act of the will so that the pain of that memory can no longer control you.) Speak to them as though you and they are still in that old memory frame. Confess and receive forgiveness for any sin you are responsible for.
- Tell them what they did or said.
- Tell them what their actions or words caused you to believe that was not true.
- Tell them the truth that you have now heard from the Lord Himself.

How do you see those who wounded you in the memory frame now in relation to the Lord's presence? Describe it here.

_____

_____

_____

_____

_____

Now revisit the recent situation you cited at the beginning of this exercise. How do you see it now in light of what God has shown you?

_____

_____

_____

_____

_____

Now that you have received truth and healing, past and present, command all unclean spirits who took advantage of open doors to depart in the name of Jesus Christ. Tell them the truth then tell them to go!

_____

_____

_____

_____

What was true in the past is true in the present and will be God's promise to you in the future.

The truth in the past was: _____

_____

The truth in the present is: _____

_____

God's promise to me for the future is: _____

_____

Lighting

What has the Lord revealed to you concerning His presence and healing truth that He brought to your wounded memories? Note how He expressed His presence to you in the memory picture. Write down what that expression has taught you about God.

_____

_____

_____

_____

_____

_____

Choose one or more of the Scriptures listed at the end of the "Learning" section and personalize them by writing them out here, substituting your name in the text. Soak in the truth that God has spoken to you—make it real in your life.

_____

_____

_____

_____

_____

_____

_____

_____

_____

_____

_____

_____

_____

_____

_____

_____

_____

_____

_____

_____

_____

_____

Chapter Twelve

STARING INTO EMPTINESS

Jebusites: The Influence of Hopelessness

Reading assignment: Chapter Twelve, pages 143-156.

Please read the Scripture text, John 20:11-18.

Learning

1. The chief lie of hopelessness is "I will never...." Hope is the thing that keeps us moving forward toward some positive expectation. Our hope and vision is based on our understanding. *Never* is the operative word of hopelessness.

2. Hoping and seeing go together. We hope for what we see. When we can no longer see, we no longer hope. We become hopeless.

3. Those who live under the influence of hopelessness frequently feel...

    *   Cursed
    *   Defeated
    *   Depressed
    *   Negative
    *   Tired
    *   Empty
    *   Indifferent
    *   Pessimistic
    *   Suicidal
    *   Disappointed

    There may be other similar words that describe how you feel.

4. The effect of hopelessness is to simply quit. It is as though we are in a row boat moving into a fog. When we can no longer see ahead we just give up and stop rowing. We sit in the fog and wait for

something bad to happen. When we can't see or understand, we don't move ahead.

5.   The truth about hopelessness:
   •   Our hope is alive.
   Blessed be the God and Father of our Lord Jesus Christ, who according to His great mercy has caused us to be born again to a living hope through the resurrection of Jesus Christ from the dead (1 Peter 1:3).

   •   Our hope is in greater revelation of a Person: Jesus Christ.
   Mary had been delivered of seven devils—she was still hopeless.
   Mary heard the teaching—she was still hopeless.
   Mary had seen countless miracles—she was still hopeless.
   Mary was at the foot of the cross—she was still hopeless.
   Mary saw an empty tomb—she was still hopeless.
   Mary saw the angels—she was still hopeless.

   And now, Lord, for what do I wait? My hope is in You (Psalm 39:7).

   And everyone who has this hope fixed on Him purifies himself, just as He is pure (1 John 3:3).

   •   The character of God is the collateral of our hope.

   Then the Lord passed by in front of him and proclaimed, "The Lord, the Lord God, compassionate and gracious, slow to anger, and abounding in lovingkindness and truth; who keeps lovingkindness for thousands, who forgives iniquity, transgression and sin...(Exodus 34:6-7).

Living

Step 1: What do you feel?

How does the picture of Mary staring into the empty tomb compare with your life? Are there times you just want to lay down and quit? Do you feel cursed, doomed, defeated, resigned, pessimistic, negative, disappointed, empty, depressed or anything like these? Describe similarities of your life and the experiences of Mary Magdalene in the box below.

_____

_____

Step 2: When do you feel it?

Can you describe a recent time when you felt the things described above? Write a brief description in the picture frame below. Before you begin to write, acknowledge the presence and involvement of God through prayer. Do not proceed until you have bathed in prayer and His presence. Declare the intention of the Lord to bring you truth and healing and forbid any lies or interference from unclean spirits.

Describe what you were feeling in that recent event.

_____

_____

_____

_____

_____

Step 3: Where did these feelings come from?

Now, pray that the Lord would lead you to the source of those feelings. Ask Him to take you by the hand and lead you to a memory that feels like the recent event you described. Describe the memory picture in the frame below as you did with the recent event. (Note that there may be more than one. Try to find the oldest memory or the one that stands out the most.)

_____

_____

_____

_____

_____

As you look at the memory frame, ask the Lord to fill it with His presence. Don't move on to the next step until you have begun to experience the presence of God in this frame.

Step 4: What is the truth?

Once you have begun to experience the presence of God, ask yourself the following questions.

- **What** do you feel as you look at this memory frame?

As I look at this memory frame I feel...

_____

_____

_____

_____

- **Why** do you feel that way? The "*why*" is the lie.

I feel what I feel because...

_____

_____

_____

_____

Ask the Lord to *express* His presence in that memory frame. Describe how you experience the presence of the Lord (i.e. feelings, impressions, pictures, etc.). One easy way to do this is to see the memory frame as a painting. How is the Lord painting Himself into the picture? What is He doing—saying—expressing—gesturing to you as you focus on Him?

_____

_____

_____

_____

- What does the Lord seem to be telling you about the truth of that situation through the expression of His presence, words, feelings, pictures, etc.?

I felt _____

because I believed _____.

But the truth is _____.

- Clean the house. Forgive or receive forgiveness associated with the memory. Forgive and release those who wounded you. (Remember that forgiveness is not an act of emotion, but an act of the will so that the pain of that memory can no longer control you.) Speak to them as though you and they are still in that old memory frame. Confess and receive forgiveness for any sin you are responsible for.
- Tell them what they did or said.
- Tell them what their actions or words caused you to believe that was not true.
- Tell them the truth that you have now heard from the Lord Himself.

How do you see those who wounded you in the memory frame now in relation to the Lord's presence? Describe it here.

_____

_____

_____

_____

_____

Now revisit the recent situation you cited at the beginning of this exercise. How do you see it now in light of what God has shown you?

_____

_____

_____

_____

_____

Now that you have received truth and healing, past and present, command all unclean spirits who took advantage of open doors to depart in the name of Jesus Christ. Tell them the truth then tell them to go!

_____

_____

_____

_____

What was true in the past is true in the present and will be God's promise to you in the future.

The truth in the past was: _____

_____

The truth in the present is: _____

_____

God's promise to me for the future is: _____

_____

Lighting

What has the Lord revealed to you concerning His presence and healing truth that He brought to your wounded memories? Note how He expressed His presence to you in the memory picture. Write down what that expression has taught you about God.

_____

_____

_____

_____

_____

_____

_____

Choose one or more of the Scriptures listed at the end of the "Learn-ing" section and personalize them by writing them out here, substituting your name in the text. Soak in the truth that God has spoken to you—make it real in your life.

_____

_____

_____

_____

_____

_____

_____

_____

_____

_____

_____

_____

_____

_____

_____

_____

_____

_____

_____

_____

_____

_____

Part III

WALKING IN THE TRUTH

Chapter Thirteen

To Be Continued....

So Jesus was saying to those Jews who had believed Him, "If you continue in My word, then you are truly disciples of Mine; and you will know the truth, and the truth will make you free" (John 8:31-32).

You have walked through much teaching and truth as you worked through the *Altars of the Heart Personal Ministry Guide*. New beliefs have been planted and old painful lies replaced. Now those new truths must be walked out in your life.

In the Gospel of John, Jesus told those who had come to new understanding that they now had to "continue" in His word. To continue is simply to make truth a part of our lives. It's kind of like rebooting a computer with a new operating system. Every part of life will now be operating out of a basis of new information.

Jesus told His new followers in John 8 that they had to continue in His word, and that would lead them to experience truth. Truth must also become true to us personally as we walk it out. As they came to a new experiential knowledge of the truth they would find even more freedom. "You will know the truth, and the truth will make you free" (Jn. 8:32).

In the same way, you must now continue in the truth you have received and thereby become free. We are providing additional scriptural truth for you to soak in as you continue in the truth. Remember that the greatest truth is the presence of the Lord Himself. Jesus is Truth in the flesh.

What follows is a topical list of Scriptures that will reinforce the truths you have received. Read them—meditate on them—soak them in. You will be given space to journal whatever the Lord brings to you as you meditate on His Word. Don't just read words, but rather see what you are reading. Allow the written Word *of* God to become the personal Word *from* God to you.

Following this section there will be space for you to journal the truth and revelation you have received. Journaling is important because it gives us a way to accumulate the truth of God. There will be additional space to record anxious thoughts that can be subjected to the truth you have received. It is important to process these anxious thoughts that are loaded with falsehoods and half truths. You are not responsible for any thought that is not from God. This section will give you the opportunity to take those thoughts captive and bring them into line with what is true in Christ.

The Healing Truth

I suggest you confess these Scriptures by personalizing them, substituting your name in them for those God is blessing, protecting, etc.

- *Fear—You are not alone; Christ is with you.*

Behold, I am with you and will keep you wherever you go, and will bring you back to this land; for I will not leave you until I have done what I have promised you (Genesis 28:15).

Be strong and courageous, do not be afraid or tremble at them, for the Lord your God is the one who goes with you. He will not fail you or forsake you (Deuteronomy 31:6).

Have I not commanded you? Be strong and courageous! Do not tremble or be dismayed, for the Lord your God is with you wherever you go (Joshua 1:9).

The Lord of hosts is with us; the God of Jacob is our stronghold (Psalm 46:7).

Be strong and courageous, do not fear or be dismayed because of the king of Assyria nor because of all the horde that is with him; for the one with us is greater than the one with him (2 Chronicles 32:7).

But now, thus says the Lord, your Creator, O Jacob, and He who formed you, O Israel, "Do not fear, for I have redeemed you; I have called you by name; you are Mine! When you pass through the waters, I will be with you; and through the rivers, they will not overflow you. When you walk through the fire, you will not be scorched, nor will the flame burn you" (Isaiah 43:1-2).

- *Rejection—You are accepted in Christ.*

They will say of Me, "Only in the Lord are righteousness and strength." Men will come to Him, and all who were angry at Him will be put to shame. In the Lord all the offspring of Israel will be justified and will glory (Isaiah 45:24-25).

In His days Judah will be saved, and Israel will dwell securely; and this is His name by which He will be called, "The Lord our righteousness" (Jeremiah 23:6).

For all have sinned and fall short of the glory of God, being justified as a gift by His grace through the redemption which is in Christ Jesus (Romans 3:23-24).

For the kingdom of God is not eating and drinking, but righteousness and peace and joy in the Holy Spirit. For he who in this way serves Christ is acceptable to God and approved by men (Romans 14:17-18).

Having predestined us to adoption as sons by Jesus Christ to Himself, according to the good pleasure of His will, to the praise of the glory of His grace, by which He has made us accepted in the Beloved (Ephesians 1:5-6 NKJ).

- *Worthlessness—You are approved in Christ, handmade and precious.*

God created man in His own image, in the image of God He created him; male and female He created them (Genesis 1:27).

Know that the Lord Himself is God; it is He who has made us, and not we ourselves; we are His people and the sheep of His pasture (Psalm 100:3).

Your hands made me and fashioned me; give me understanding, that I may learn Your commandments (Psalm 119:73).

For You formed my inward parts; You wove me in my mother's womb. I will give thanks to You, for I am fearfully and wonderfully made; wonderful are Your works, and my soul knows it very well (Psalm 139:13-14).

The people whom I formed for Myself will declare My praise (Isaiah 43:21).

But by the grace of God I am what I am... (1 Corinthians 15:10).

Therefore if anyone is in Christ, he is a new creature; the old things passed away; behold, new things have come (2 Corinthians 5:17).

For we are His workmanship, created in Christ Jesus for good works, which God prepared beforehand so that we would walk in them (Ephesians 2:10).

Do not lie to one another, since you laid aside the old self with its evil practices, and have put on the new self who is being renewed to a true knowledge according to the image of the One who created him (Colossians 3:9-10).

- Shame—You are clothed with Christ.

How blessed is he whose transgression is forgiven, whose sin is covered! (Psalm 32:1)

For all of you who were baptized into Christ have clothed yourselves with Christ (Galatians 3:27).

I will rejoice greatly in the Lord, my soul will exult in my God; for He has clothed me with garments of salvation, He has wrapped me with a robe of righteousness (Isaiah 61:10a).

But put on the Lord Jesus Christ, and make no provision for the flesh in regard to its lusts (Romans 13:14).

- Insecurity—You are safe and secure in Christ.

The eternal God is a dwelling place, and underneath are the everlasting arms (Deuteronomy 33:27a).

O Lord, how my adversaries have increased! Many are rising up against me. Many are saying of my soul, "There is no deliverance for him in God." Selah. But You, O Lord, are a shield about me, my glory, and the One who lifts my head (Psalm 3:1-3).

Many are the sorrows of the wicked, but he who trusts in the Lord, lovingkindness shall surround him (Psalm 32:10).

The angel of the Lord encamps around those who fear Him, and rescues them (Psalm 34:7).

The Lord is your keeper; the Lord is your shade on your right hand. The sun will not smite you by day, nor the moon by night. The Lord will protect you from all evil; He will keep your soul. The Lord will guard your going out and your coming in from this time forth and forever (Psalm 121:5-8).

Those who trust in the Lord are as Mount Zion, which cannot be moved but abides forever. As the mountains surround Jerusalem, so the Lord surrounds His people from this time forth and forever (Psalm 125:1-2).

My sheep hear My voice, and I know them, and they follow Me; and I give eternal life to them, and they will never perish; and no one will snatch them out of My hand. My Father, who has given them to Me, is greater than all; and no one is able to snatch them out of the Father's hand (John 10:27-29).

• *Defilement—You are washed and restored in Christ.*

O God, restore us and cause Your face to shine upon us, and we will be saved (Psalm 80:3).

"For I will restore you to health and I will heal you of your wounds," declares the Lord, "Because they have called you an outcast, saying: 'It is Zion; no one cares for her' " (Jeremiah 30:17).

"Then I passed by you and saw you, and behold, you were at the time for love; so I spread My skirt over you and covered your nakedness. I also swore to you and entered into a covenant with you so that you became Mine," declares the Lord God (Ezekiel 16:8).

Also I will restore the captivity of My people Israel, and they will rebuild the ruined cities and live in them; they will also plant vineyards and drink their wine, and make gardens and eat their fruit (Amos 9:14).

For the Lord will restore the splendor of Jacob like the splendor of Israel, even though devastators have devastated them and destroyed their vine branches (Nahum 2:2).

• *Hopelessness—You have a new and living hope in Christ.*

O Israel, hope in the Lord; for with the Lord there is lovingkindness, and with Him is abundant redemption (Psalm 130:7).

For in hope we have been saved, but hope that is seen is not hope; for who hopes for what he already sees? But if we hope for what we do not see, with perseverance we wait eagerly for it (Romans 8:24-25).

Blessed be the God and Father of our Lord Jesus Christ, who according to His great mercy has caused us to be born again to a living hope through the resurrection of Jesus Christ from the dead, to obtain an inheritance which is imperishable and undefiled and will not fade away, reserved in heaven for you, who are protected by the power of God through faith for a salvation ready to be revealed in the last time (1 Peter 1:3-5).

Therefore, prepare your minds for action, keep sober in spirit, fix your hope completely on the grace to be brought to you at the revelation of Jesus Christ (1 Peter 1:13).

And everyone who has this hope fixed on Him purifies himself, just as He is pure (1 John 3:3).

There are many other Scriptures that could be added to these. I urge you to search them out. Read His words and allow them to draw you into His presence. Hear His voice and know Him.

Truth Journal

What truths has the Lord revealed to you as you walked through this book? Take time to walk back through the pages of this book and the notes you have made. Notice how the Lord has added to your revelation of Him. The greater your revelation of God, the greater your healing will be. Healing, like our revelation of God, happens over a period of time. I urge you to revisit this section many times to remind yourself what the Lord has personally spoken to you. Get another notebook to journal what God continues to add to your personal revelation of Him.

Once lies and obstacles have been removed you can expect greater intimacy with the Lord. This book is not the end, but the beginning of new, intimate hearing of God. Call upon Him—respond to His gentle invitation to you to hear Him.

"Call to Me and I will answer you, and I will tell you great and mighty things, which you do not know" (Jeremiah 33:3).

My Anxious Thoughts

The instructions here are simple. When something happens that causes some kind of strong emotional response in you, write it down here. Then write what you felt about that event and why you felt that way. Then invite the presence of the Lord and simply ask Him what is true.

What happened?

_____

_____

_____

What did you feel about the event?

_____

_____

_____

Why did you feel that way? (This is your belief about the event.)

_____

_____

_____

_____

Ask the Lord, "Lord, what is the truth about this event?

_____

_____

_____

_____

What happened?

_____

_____

_____

_____

_____

What did you feel about the event?

_____

_____

_____

_____

_____

Why did you feel that way? (This is your belief about the event.)

_____

_____

_____

_____

_____

Ask the Lord, "Lord, what is the truth about this event?

_____

_____

_____

_____

_____

What happened?

_____

_____

_____

_____

_____

What did you feel about the event?

_____

_____

_____

_____

_____

Why did you feel that way? (This is your belief about the event.)

_____

_____

_____

_____

_____

Ask the Lord, "Lord, what is the truth about this event?

_____

_____

_____

_____

_____

What happened?

_____

_____

_____

_____

_____

What did you feel about the event?

_____

_____

_____

_____

_____

Why did you feel that way? (This is your belief about the event.)

_____

_____

_____

_____

_____

Ask the Lord, "Lord, what is the truth about this event?

_____

_____

_____

_____

_____

What happened?

_____

_____

_____

_____

_____

What did you feel about the event?

_____

_____

_____

_____

_____

Why did you feel that way? (This is your belief about the event.)

_____

_____

_____

_____

_____

Ask the Lord, "Lord, what is the truth about this event?

_____

_____

_____

_____

_____

What happened?

_____

_____

_____

_____

_____

What did you feel about the event?

_____

_____

_____

_____

_____

Why did you feel that way? (This is your belief about the event.)

_____

_____

_____

_____

_____

Ask the Lord, "Lord, what is the truth about this event?

_____

_____

_____

_____

_____

What happened?

_____

_____

_____

_____

_____

What did you feel about the event?

_____

_____

_____

_____

Why did you feel that way? (This is your belief about the event.)

_____

_____

_____

_____

Ask the Lord, "Lord, what is the truth about this event?

_____

_____

_____

_____

_____

What happened?

_____

_____

_____

_____

_____

What did you feel about the event?

_____

_____

_____

_____

_____

Why did you feel that way? (This is your belief about the event.)

_____

_____

_____

_____

_____

Ask the Lord, "Lord, what is the truth about this event?

_____

_____

_____

_____

_____

What happened?

_____

_____

_____

_____

_____

What did you feel about the event?

_____

_____

_____

_____

_____

Why did you feel that way? (This is your belief about the event.)

_____

_____

_____

_____

_____

Ask the Lord, "Lord, what is the truth about this event?

_____

_____

_____

_____

_____

What happened?

_____

_____

_____

_____

_____

What did you feel about the event?

_____

_____

_____

_____

_____

Why did you feel that way? (This is your belief about the event.)

_____

_____

_____

_____

_____

Ask the Lord, "Lord, what is the truth about this event?

_____

_____

_____

_____

_____

REFERENCES

Biblesoft's New Exhaustive Strong's Numbers and Concordance with Expanded Greek-Hebrew Dictionary. 1994. Biblesoft and International Bible Translators, Inc.

Crabb, Larry. 1977. *Effective Biblical Counseling.* Grand Rapids, MI: Zondervan Publishing House.

Flynn, Mike, and Doug Gregg. 1993. *Inner Healing.* Downers Grove, IL: Intervarsity Press.

Kraft, Charles H. 1993. *Deep Wounds, Deep Healing.* Ann Arbor, MI: Servant Pub.

Long, Brad, and Cindy Strickler. 2001. *Let Jesus Heal Your Hidden Wounds.* Grand Rapids, MI: Chosen Books.

Petersen, Alice; Gary Sweeten; and Dorothy Faye Geverdt. 1990. "Renewing Mind." *Rational Christian Thinking.* Cincinnati: Equipping Ministries Int'l.

Sandford, John, and Paula Sandford. 1985. *Healing the Wounded Spirit.* Tulsa, OK: Victory House, Inc.

Sandford, John Loren, and Mark Sandford. 1992. *A Comprehensive Guide to Deliverance and Healing.* Grand Rapids, MI: Chosen Books.

Seamands, David A. 1985. *Healing of Memories.* Colorado Springs, CO: Chariot Victor Pub.

Smith, Edward M. 2002. *Beyond Tolerable Recovery.* Campbellsville, KY: Family Care Pub.

THOM GARDNER

Altars of the Heart and
Altars of the Heart Personal Ministry Guide

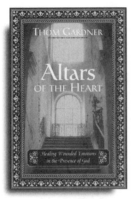

0-7684-3009-7

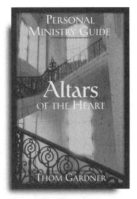

0-7684-3020-8

Altars of the Heart is a living and healing picture that wraps powerful expositions of the Word around the lives of real people. The compelling hope of the book flows from the hearts of many people who have been healed from emotional pain by the presence of the Lord.

Gardner exposes negative emotions such as fear, rejection, worthlessness, shame, insecurity, defilement, and hopelessness that prevent us from living in the grace and peace God intends for us. You will walk through a gentle process, uncovering lies embedded in your emotional wounds and discovering peace and truth in the presence of the Living Christ. *Altars of the Heart* will bring you to a new sense of intimate closeness with God as it leads you to a healing place in the heart of God.

Additional copies of this book and other
book titles from DESTINY IMAGE are
available at your local bookstore.

For a complete list of our titles,
visit us at www.destinyimage.com
Send a request for a catalog to:

Destiny Image® Publishers, Inc.

P.O. Box 310
Shippensburg, PA 17257-0310

*"Speaking to the Purposes of God for This
Generation and for the Generations to Come"*